STONE GATHERING

A READER

STONE GATHERING

A READER

poems, small fictions, essayettes

DEBORAH JACOBS, SERIES EDITOR

Stone Gathering

A Reader

Volume Two, Issue Two   Fall 2020

Layout and Design by Chip & Jean Borkenhagen, River Place Press, Aitkin, MN

Cover Photo: Joey Halvorson Photography

Printed at Bang Printing, Brainerd, MN

ISBN: 978-1-7347600-3-3

First Edition

An imprint of
Danielle Dufy Literary

P.O. Box 334
Brainerd, MN 56401
www.danielledufy.com

Dedicated
to the memories of

George Floyd
(1973-2020)

and

Representative John Lewis
(1940-2020)

Black Lives Matter

Contents

Contents

CONTENTS

Before you learn the tender gravity of kindness
you must travel where the Indian in a white poncho
lies dead by the side of the road.
You must see how this could be you,
how he too was someone
who journeyed through the night with plans
and the simple breath that kept him alive.

—Naomi Shihab Nye (from "Kindness")

Introduction

I had hoped to be editing this Fall 2020 issue of *Stone Gathering* in a post pandemic world, or at least in one where the pandemic's end was in sight. And yet, here we are—with everyone from publishers to permissions people to contributors still working remotely and, let's admit it, not perhaps at their most passionate, most focused, most energized best. I'm certainly not. Everybody, it seems, moves more tentatively these days, by default or by choice.

For my part, I'm dutifully cranking out each of the promised five issues per year, even though they mostly have nowhere to go. I am deeply grateful for subscribers and a few fiercely committed booksellers who somehow keep ordering, even though most bookstores aren't open to browsing. But I miss the pleasure and privilege of promoting *Stone Gathering* publicly and in person, primarily through *gatherings*, which is how it gained such strong momentum and how, I hope, it one day regains it.

The upside to less travel and fewer—I mean, zero—events is this: I've had a lot of time to ponder things. I'm reassessing the website, for instance (and pardon its bare bones while it gets a design make-over). I am also reconsidering my heretofore antipathetic relationship to *Zoom* and other online gathering places, a rethinking made easier now that I have great internet service for the first time in 20 years.

But what's been most on my mind these last few months is this: whether I am doing enough to further *Stone Gathering*'s mission to reach a wider audience. I am not! And that exclamation point was put there on May 25th, when George Floyd was murdered by a Minneapolis police officer. I always describe the contents of *Stone Gathering* as a gift of short literature that *matters*, as words people *need to hear*. Well right now people, all people, need to hear more Black voices—in *Stone Gathering* and everywhere else.

And so, it was an uncanny confluence of things when, on May 25th, my renewed resolve to do more coincided with a stalled-out gathering process (and several unfilled spots), which made room for more Black voices—not in the next issue or some nebulous time in the future, but right now, in this Fall issue.

From the beginning, I have tried to collect disparate voices in *Stone Gathering*. The world is simply a better place when there are more voices in the room. Going forward, I hope a wider range of readers can see themselves in these pages; I hope they will find more short literature that matters to *their* lives because we all need that. But it won't happen until White publishers like me, especially those of us who hold out hope for a more racially just future, adamantly resist envisioning their audiences as primarily White. It's a big deal. Let's get busy.

Stay safe. Be well. Have hope.

Deborah Jacobs, Nisswa MN

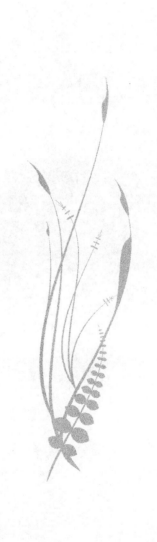

A Small Needful Fact

by Ross Gay

Is that Eric Garner worked
for some time for the Parks and Rec.
Horticultural Department, which means,
perhaps, that with his very large hands,
perhaps, in all likelihood,
he put gently into the earth
some plants which, most likely,
some of them, in all likelihood,
continue to grow, continue
to do what such plants do, like house
and feed small and necessary creatures,
like being pleasant to touch and smell,
like converting sunlight
into food, like making it easier
for us to breathe.

Being 17 in Bismarck, North Dakota

by Siri Liv Myhrom

I was born in a tropical heat on an island skimmed by equator. I arrived fat and pale-skinned, with hair so blonde it shone pearly under the high sun.

We were the only white people in our neighborhood, though of course Papua New Guinea was no stranger to white folks in 1976. By then, there had already been over 100 years of colonization and just one year of independence.

Occasionally, my mother said, the Papuans—some with skin so dark it glimmered blue under the high sun—would take their thumb and rub my forehead, to see if the color was real, if there was something darker underneath.

I was a novelty, a kind of doll, a chunky toddler who ate spiders and whom the house girl, Anna, rushed out to rescue when she spotted from the kitchen window a great venomous brown snake coiling its way towards me under the towering rain tree.

One day, so the story goes, when I was three, I decided to visit my dad at the university. So I walked out our front door while my mother was occupied with my older brother, meandering oblivious across the busy Waigani Drive, until I got to the nearby campus, asking everyone where my dad was. Finally, two uni students who knew him picked me up and took me to his office. He was stunned, to say the least.

These are not memories, of course, only stories. Re-told, re-framed, all the genuine terror edited out so there is a kind of breathless heroism and fish-out-of-water hilarity to them. We left Papua New Guinea when I was almost six. I have no memory of fear, no memory of being different, only special, a towheaded darling plucked from danger at every turn.

I don't remember ever thinking about skin color. We didn't really talk about it as a family, though I knew racism was bad. When I was 16 and went on a service trip to Minneapolis, I bought a t-shirt at the mall that said Love Sees No Color. In my heart, I believed that was real.

George Floyd was murdered about a mile from our house. The world cracked open, and what has come gushing out of that global wound has shaken me. I learned not to hate—that much is true enough—and in my adult life I've even been involved with racial justice organizations and efforts. But I also somewhere learned that it was unnecessary for me to pay too much attention —to real history, to the ways the most deadly things about us can be so quiet. Where did I learn that? I don't remember.

I do remember being 17 in Bismarck, North Dakota, and my mother sending me to the grocery store. I remember being in the cereal aisle, but I don't remember taking notice of a black man approaching from the opposite end. The only reason I knew there was a black man was because I heard him say, "You don't have to grab your purse, lady. I'm not going to steal it." I looked up, and he passed by. And I looked down, and there was my hand, clutching my purse in the seat of the cart, where my hand had not been before. I was embarrassed, quietly defensive, already making rationalizations on the drive home.

It's taken me 25 years to see the line, a thin filament, easily explained away as a trick of the eye, a misunderstanding, that connects that moment in the grocery store to the moment of George's neck under a heavy knee. It feels plain to me now, not a statement of my goodness or badness, but just a fact, a simple true thing from which to start a long walk. Stories of goodness and badness, ours and others', are just places to hide out, like the kind of obliviousness that leads to chronic forgetting. I am no longer a three year old, wobbling through zooming intersections, counting on being kept safe, delivered by others to my destination. I am unwilling to edit, and I am unwilling to forget.

jasper texas 1998

by Lucille Clifton
for j. byrd

i am a man's head hunched in the road.
i was chosen to speak by the members
of my body. the arm as it pulled away
pointed toward me, the hand opened once
and was gone.

why and why and why
should i call a white man brother?
who is the human in this place,
the thing that is dragged or the dragger?
what does my daughter say?

the sun is a blister overhead.
if i were alive i could not bear it.
the townsfolk sing we shall overcome
while hope bleeds slowly from my mouth
into the dirt that covers us all.
i am done with this dust. i am done.

Chestnut

by Rebecca Baggett

I touched a chestnut sapling
in the Georgia mountains.

My friend writes of the great trees
and their vanishing,

but I have seen a young chestnut,
tender and green, rising from its ashes.

I, too, write of loss and grief,
the hollow they carve

in the chest,
but that hollow may shelter

some new thing,
a life I could not

have imagined or wished,
a life I would never

have chosen. I have seen
the chestnut rising,

luminous,
from its own bones,

from the ash of its first life.

Renewal

by Christopher DeWan

She buried her husband with thirty-two years of *National Geographic* back issues on top of his coffin. Once, he'd sworn the magazines would leave the house "Over my dead body!" and when he passed, she granted his wish. The new emptiness of the basement bookshelf was like the new emptiness in her life: it was odd and unexpected, and she wasn't quite sure yet how to fill it; but she knew she'd find a way.

Autumn Beside the River

by Rosemerry Wahtola Trommer

The rocks that were underwater
two months ago are dry now,
and a woman can sit on them
beneath the bridge and escape
the September sun. But she can't
escape herself. There was a time
she really believed she could control things.
Now she sits with her own brokenness
and invites the inevitable autumn into her,
the autumn that's already come.
Invites the lengthening nights. Invites
the dank scent of the garden, moldering and dead.
Invites the loss of green. *You can't be
a sapling forever*, she tells herself,
though another part of her argues,
Yes you can, yes you can.

The river has never been so clear—
every rock in the bed is visible now,
and perhaps clarity is one of autumn's best gifts.
She imagines the leaves of her falling off—
how she loves them.
She imagines them golden in the wind.

Bullet Points

by Jericho Brown

I will not shoot myself
In the head, and I will not shoot myself
In the back, and I will not hang myself
With a trashbag, and if I do,
I promise you, I will not do it
In a police car while handcuffed
Or in the jail cell of a town
I only know the name of
Because I have to drive through it
To get home. Yes, I may be at risk,
But I promise you, I trust the maggots
Who live beneath the floorboards
Of my house to do what they must
To any carcass more than I trust
An officer of the law of the land
To shut my eyes like a man
Of God might, or to cover me with a sheet
So clean my mother could have used it
To tuck me in. When I kill me, I will
Do it the same way most Americans do,
I promise you: cigarette smoke
Or a piece of meat on which I choke
Or so broke I freeze
In one of these winters we keep

Calling worst. I promise if you hear
Of me dead anywhere near
A cop, then that cop killed me. He took
Me from us and left my body, which is,
No matter what we've been taught,
Greater than the settlement
A city can pay a mother to stop crying,
And more beautiful that the new bullet
Fished from the folds of my brain.

My Friend Barb, Our Neighbor George

by Michael Kleber-Diggs

Before the pandemic, before I worked from home, I knew my neighbor, Barb, tended her lawn herself. I knew she mowed her grass, pulled weeds by hand, applied fertilizer where it was needed, and got down on her knees to dig up and reseed any rough patches. But before I saw her work all day, I didn't know she did.

Barb is closer to 90 than 80. She is sprite-like and charming. We talk about the weather or trees or our dogs or her-late husband, Bob, or, when we're feeling catty, other neighbors—interesting gossip sometimes, never anything mean-spirited.

A few years ago, very early in the morning, a woman, a white woman, an intoxicated white woman rifled through my wife's truck, stood at our front window with a heavy rock above her head ready to throw it through, rang our doorbell several times, shouted profanities at us and demanded to be let in. We yelled at her to go, but I did not leave my house to confront her until she left our front porch and walked toward Barb and Bob's house. She didn't stop to bother Bob and Barb. She walked down the alley and disappeared into darkness.

Barb's lawn is perfect. She mows twice a week. I know that now. She whacks tall grass around trees and streetlight posts. She trims the edges every time. When she isn't mowing, she's weeding. She works on her yard every day.

I don't why Barb's lawn matters to her. I don't know if she loves

28

yard work or does it to honor Bob, for exercise, or for some other reason. I know she isn't motivated by what her neighbors think. Everyone around her does just enough yard work to avoid complaints. I only know her lawn is important to her.

This has been a cruel summer. The pandemic has brought a persistent nervousness to the world. George Floyd was killed in Minneapolis, ten miles away from Barb's house and mine. If you don't understand what it's like to be Black in America, if you don't know how it feels for many Blacks in the days and months after the police kill a Black man or woman, I write to tell you the hard part has not started yet. For all who feel these killings personally, the hard part is just beginning.

George Floyd's character will be called into question. His humanity will be called into question—quiet suggestions he deserved to be tortured to death. Those who can, will return to normal routines. Pro-police and anti-protestor messages will increase. People won't make a sincere effort to engage with suggestions for reform. If the name of the movement isn't just right, many will opt out without checking it out. Any urgency the white community feels toward action, any efforts to look inward, to work for real change, any efforts now underway, may succumb to the status quo. Racism never left. It went dormant for a few days. It will crawl back into our city life like a weed.

I thought a long time about centering my friend Barb instead of George Floyd. I thought about my audience. I wanted to share three ideas—one aspirational, one metaphorical, one spiritual.

First, people like the woman who visited us early in the morning need help and grace, not brutality and violence.

Second, the work of building the world we claim to want - the work of ending racism—that work is daily work. Each of us must value the work. Our inspiration should be internal, not external; it should come from within each of us.

My last idea is applied in the first idea and is expressed in the work of the second, my last idea is about George and Barb and unwanted early morning visitors and you and me and Minneapolis and Saint Paul and America and so on. My last idea is this: we are meant to love our neighbors.

The Tally

by Marvin Bell

Along with my Tom Mix decoder badge had come a small booklet showing the many places on his body Tom Mix had been injured. He had done most of it to himself, stunts for his movies. The chart covered broken bones, ruptured joints and torn tendons, but not heartaches or regrets. Nor errors of commission or omission. When Dorothy's mother was dying in southern Illinois, no one would give up a plane seat for Dorothy to get there in time. Without someone to blame, the event rests in between what someone could have done and what they failed to do. If I look back, I wonder what my father and I would have talked about had he lived longer. Would-haves and should-haves? We were not given to analysis, least of all self-analysis. Our era was an Age of "None of Your Business" and "Suck It Up." Young men who erred were not sent to jail but to the military. Most crimes were handled off the books. Good deeds were done in private, no one need know. How, in the welter of years, can one "be there" for everyone for whom one has felt affection? My list of friends and good acquaintances who have passed away is nearing two hundred. I still know them. I liked one, I helped one, I failed one—take your pick. Only the wholly selfish have no regrets. A tally of our errors is fodder for biographers, but I remain more amazed at how much goes right. My favorite cartoon is of a man in an easy chair holding a newspaper open to the obits on which the individual headlines read, TWENTY YEARS YOUNGER THAN YOU... FIFTEEN YEARS YOUNGER THAN YOU... THIRTY YEARS YOUNGER THAN YOU. *Carpe diem* means not looking back. But we do.

Lord, Help Me Be Like The Knitters

by Amy Baskin

There is as much of a chance that the world will end today as there ever has been and god knows that Shiva's wheel of destruction is spinning full bore right now.

But that doesn't stop the six ladies at the next table from holding their two-hour knitting circle this morning at this cafe, rain or shine.

All threats and possible endings and Armageddon aside, they actually called in to book the largest table in the coffee house in advance.

This is the bravest act I am aware of today. They have their steady gig, their weekly commitment to attendance.

This is how to give zero fucks. Readers sliding down the bridges of each nose. The occasional smart-ass crack, the furious clack of needles, the skeins of brightly dyed wool.

When one falls and rolls across the floor, another calmly leans down to pick up.

The Hawk

by Brian Doyle

Recently a man took up residence on my town's football field, sleeping in a small tent in the northwestern corner, near the copse of cedars. He had been a terrific football player some years ago for our high school, and then had played in college, and then a couple of years in the nether reaches of the professional ranks, where a man might get paid a hundred bucks a game plus bonuses for touchdowns and sacks. Then he had entered into several business ventures, but these had not gone so well, and he had married and had children, but that had not gone so well either, and finally he'd taken up residence on the football field, because, he said, that was where things had gone well, and he sort of needed to get balanced again, and there was something about the field that was working for him, as far as he could tell. So, with all due respect to people who thought he was a nutcase, he decided he would stay there until someone made him leave. He had already spoken with the cops, and it was a mark of the general decency of our town that he was told he could stay as long as he didn't interfere with use of the field, which of course he would never think of doing, and it was summer, anyway, so the field wasn't in use much.

He had been nicknamed the Hawk when he was a player, for his habit of lurking around almost lazily on defense and then making a stunning strike, and he still speaks the way he played, quietly but then amazingly. When we sat on the visiting team's bench the other day, he said some quietly amazing things, which I think you should hear:

The reporter from the paper came by, he said. She wanted to write a story about the failure of the American dream and the collapse of the social contract, and she was just melting to use football as a metaphor for something or other, and I know she was just trying to do her job, but I kept telling her things that didn't fit what she wanted, like that people come by and leave me cookies and sandwiches, and the kids who play lacrosse at night set up a screen so my tent won't get peppered by stray shots, and the cops drift by at night to make sure no one's giving me grief. Everyone gets nailed at some point, so we understand someone getting nailed and trying to get back up on his feet again. I am not a drunk, and there's no politicians to blame. I just lost my balance. People are good to me. You try to get lined up again. I keep the field clean. Mostly it's discarded water bottles. Lost cellphones I hang in a plastic bag by the gate. I walk the perimeter a lot. I saw some coyote pups the other day. I don't have anything smart to say. I don't know what things mean. Things just are what they are. I never sat on the visitors' bench before, did you? Someone leaves coffee for me every morning by the gate. The other day a lady came by with twin infants, and she let me hold one while we talked about football. That baby weighed about half of nothing. You couldn't believe a human being could be so tiny —and there were two of him. That reporter, she kept asking me what I had learned, what I would say to her readers if there was only one thing I could say, and I told her, What could possibly be better than standing on a football field, holding a brand-new human being the size of a coffee cup? You know what I mean? Everything else is sort of a footnote.

Hoodie

by January Gill O'Neil

A gray hoodie will not protect my son
from rain, from the New England cold.

I see the partial eclipse of his face
as his head sinks into the half-dark

and shades his eyes. Even in our
quiet suburb with its unlocked doors,

I fear for his safety—the darkest child
on our street in the empire of blocks.

Sometimes I don't know who he is anymore
traveling the back roads between boy and man.

He strides a deep stride, pounds a basketball
into wet pavement. Will he take his shot

or is he waiting for the open-mouthed
orange rim to take a chance on him? I sing

his name to the night, ask for safe passage
from this borrowed body into the next

and wonder who could mistake him
for anything but good.

Newborn

by Danusha Laméris

The woman at the party slipped him in my arms
so she could fix herself a plate of food. Sometimes
this happens—a mother with brown skin, an island voice
will see in me her own mother, her sister,
a tributary of the blue river that runs through her veins.
But this baby was so new, his eyes still bloodshot from birth,
the red spreading like a stain through the sclera's milky white.
I held his swaddled body while he stretched those thin,
alien fingers, then clenched them back into the flannel caul.
From time to time he squinted up at me, this woman
in whose arms, for a moment, his life rested.
He did not cry, though now and then
his mouth moved in that familiar gesture of hunger.
And I did not dare sit, for fear he would disapprove,
my knees remembering the boat-like bobbing
that the new-to-land prefer. I looked down
at his squinched face, the whispered trace of eyebrows,
delicate folds of his lids, black hair, curls fine
as the whorled loops of a fingerprint,
and I wanted to whisper into his intricate ear
tell him the lie I couldn't make true:
that this is a world where he will always be safe
in the arms of a stranger. Even as he grows tall
in the darkness of his skin,

he can walk down any street, day or night,
feet scuffing the rough ground,
hands in his pockets,
his heart, whole, in his chest.

Mothers of Black Sons

by Nicole Borg

Dear Mothers of Black Sons,

I am afraid for you, your hearts.
For your teenage sons, budding young men;
your adult sons, fathers themselves.
Everyday, in your gut, the acid-fear
knowing they are not safe
are more likely to die at the hands
of white men raised on fear—
America's invasive weed, thorned
and thriving, network of old roots
so hard to pluck from fertile soils—
that makes them draw their weapons
and put your son in sights
or kneel on a bound son's neck
until he is crushed by fear's great weight.

I too have sons, light skinned brown-eyed boys.
I too have fears—car accidents,
sporting accidents, school shootings,
invisible illness silently spreading.
I do not fear my sons will be hunted
on neighborhood streets, profiled
by blue-eyed vigilantes, killed

by those in uniform. Mothers of black sons,
I try to imagine your fear, swallow the hard
pill of it, hold the enormity of it next to my heart
until it makes me sick, makes me shake,
stomach rough with storm,
chest tight with terror.

I want to clasp your hands in mine
kneel at your feet. I'm sorry.
I want to say It will end now,
with this one last black son dead
on a Minneapolis street
while onlookers tried to help
and police did not
but we both fear
that is a promise bound to break.

Jumping in Leaves

by Joseph Gross

Somewhere after the turn of the millennium I slid from leaf jumper to leaf raker, and so on this smoky November afternoon I hold down my job for the boy in front of me during what will be his only non-digital hour of the day. His blond, curly hair captures bits of maple and oak and curly strands from the hostas I raked through. "I love the fall," he says. I am surprised that he has an opinion on the season. His challenges with language and reluctance to share have long blocked us from his thoughts. He does not, I notice, say *autumn*, a word that sounds to me now like his diagnosis.

He's impressed with my raking, the way I pull and fluff from the bottom of the pile between jumps. "Good job," he says, and I feel some pride at my adult strength and leverage.

He runs laps around the yard that culminate in a cannonball or a backflop or a headfirst dive. He has shed his gloves, coat, hat, despite the forty-degree temps. I think of my own jumping age, the familiar mold and fruity cedar smell down in the pile, the desire to be buried completely.

"Cover me up!" he says, and I do. I cover him, and in this way we're almost as close as we can get, him sweaty and scratchy and hidden and hearing his own breath, me seemingly alone, leaning on my rake, the air thick from burn barrels. Both of us waiting for him to emerge.

Clementine Time

by Anna George Meek

There is no time but the time in the kitchen. My father loses track of days, and I buy a "clock" whose only hand moves from Monday to Tuesday to Wednesday, as if distinguishing between the days were important. The kitchen walls may measure a passage of time, but past and future are nothing within the space of the kitchen.

Dad is hungry for a clementine; my three-year-old daughter Sarah is hungry for a clementine. I peel one for her and feed her the wedges; my mother peels one for my father. Five minutes later, they do not remember having eaten—may they have an orange? They eat, and then they each put their sticky hands in mine. Dad grins at my mother. In any given hour, he is no more dying than Sarah is getting older. The moment is sweet and I would hold it forever. Just a clementine; then a clementine.

Clementine. Clementine.

Faraway/Nearby

by Debra Gwartney

In the modern art wing of the Metropolitan Museum, I watch a woman make her way to a bench in a dim corner. She sheds a sweater and lowers her right hand, palm flat on cool surface, before she tilts one hip and then the other, settling with a demure grunt. She reaches into a bag and pulls out a peach, maybe an apricot. A piece of fruit, anyway, the very color of the sky in Georgia O'Keeffe's *Faraway, Nearby*, which my daughter is standing next to. My oldest daughter, who rests against a rare blank space on the museum wall, leaning a bit too close to the painting. Her hip is jutted in an unconscious emulation of the antler rack in the center of the canvas, bone that looks to me sharp enough to slice skin, and her own child is twined around her body, both granddaughter and daughter staring out at who knows what.

Minutes earlier, stepping away from Egon Schiele's self-portrait—piercing eyes, twisted limbs that had mesmerized my granddaughter—we'd had words. A tense exchange because they wanted to leave and I wanted to stay. I carped in a sharper tone than I intended—*we've come such a long way, can't we forge on?* My daughter glared at this testiness. I shut my mouth and thought, well, there it is: the first fuel for an inevitable blowup between us. Indeed, it would come near the end of our trip, when it was no longer possible to hold either tongue.

Our strife is common, a mother-daughter tendency to misinterpret, to misunderstand, to jangle nerves, an old habit that nags its way into our time together no matter how brightly we set off. It's also tiresome. So I focus on the woman with the piece of fruit who sits as still as a still life. Within seconds, her three adult children—the resemblance is uncanny—flutter to her. From various points in the room, they beam toward this mother in distress. Once they circle-up, she wordlessly slips to the floor like unloosed drapery, like a silk dress unzipped and slithering to the ground. Two teenagers blend in, so now I see the woman only in flashes between the bodies of her people. I can tell she's eating the fruit, teeth sunk into flesh, pulp on her lips, while her guards watch for the museum's guard posted at the doorway, a luggish man who snaps at a visitor for using a phone to photograph the Rothko that yawns its unkempt lines across the length of the wall.

The museum guard does not view the Woman Eating a Peach. He doesn't see one of her daughters dipping toward her to wipe juice from her chin. He doesn't wonder, as I do, how this family remains devoted to their matriarch without a tinge of impatience, without any one of them seething, *Oh good god, this again?*

As I have each time I've stood in front of a piece of art, I wonder how I'm supposed to feel. Is this a quiver of envy inside me— jealousy of the woman whose every movement is attended to? Or am I leaning toward a sentiment I know well, the self-congratulatory pat I give myself for not burdening my offspring with my troubles. Because of course this isn't true: I burden them all the time and maybe doubly so when I profess I don't.

So what is it that swells in me now? Fear, I suppose. This daughter across the room: what if she fails to notice when the time comes that I must eat of the peach? What if she and her sisters aren't there to fold around me when I'm the old mother pooling to the floor in an attempt to right myself again?

I worry my daughters won't catch the bumpy stone when it falls from my mouth, as the daughter of this woman does now. She unfolds a tissue on her palm and the mother plucks the pit from her tongue and places it there, where it is wrapped tight as a cocoon. The daughter slips the bundle into her own pocket, hers to deal with now, and helps the older woman to her feet.

I nod at my own family, *let's go, it's time.* Already I sense the bustle and pinched air of New York City, the smell of perseverance and verve. We move out of the building, onto the crowded subway. We remain stiff with each other in the midst of the crowd, tight-lipped and sharp-angled, until, suddenly and without a word, my daughter slips her arm through mine, an almost innocuous gesture. I suck in my breath and squeeze her against my ribs; I hold her, her warmth, her softness, her presence. And for now, maybe it's all I need.

Butter

by Elizabeth Alexander

My mother loves butter more than I do,
more than anyone. She pulls chunks off
the stick and eats it plain, explaining
cream spun around into butter! Growing up
we ate turkey cutlets sauteed in lemon
and butter, butter and cheese on green noodles,
butter melting in small pools in the hearts
of Yorkshire puddings, butter better
than gravy staining white rice yellow,
butter glazing corn in slipping squares,
butter the lava in white volcanoes
of hominy grits, butter softening
in a white bowl to be creamed with white
sugar, butter disappearing into
whipped sweet potatoes, with pineapple,
butter melted and curdy to pour
over pancakes, butter licked off the plate
with warm Alaga syrup. When I picture
the good old days I am grinning greasy
with my brother, having watched the tiger
chase his tail and turn to butter. We are
Mumbo and Jumbo's children despite
historical revision, despite
our parent's efforts, glowing from the inside
out, one hundred megawatts of butter.

What To Do During Lockdown

by Amy Wray Irish

#7. Teach yourself a language—USA Today

First, I'll try the near-dead language
of laid-back. I'll toss out *rush* and *gotta dash*
and learn new words like *listen, hushed.*
Astonish my husband when I no longer nag;
trade *hurry up!* and *we'll be late!*
for *cozy* and *slow* and *quiet.*

Next I'll go nonverbal—the primitive tones
of my teenage son. I'll greet the creature, show
I'm not a threat with homemade pizza,
extra meat. Then start a deeper conversation
with a song that just dropped. Philosophize
with heads nodding, toes tapping, fist bumps...

Then I'll relearn my native tongue—
the vocals of play. I'll sing of itsy spiders,
rosie rings. Ropes will slap cement
and swings creak on their metal chains,
faster and faster. But most of all I'll laugh
Alongside my wisest teacher: my daughter.

And when I've practiced the language
of all in my embrace, I'll speak
to myself. Say: *you can do it*
with a stroll in the sun's warm rays; reply
I will with pen's continued scratch.
Each day I'll talk to me and promise

I'll walk a little further; write
a little more; and always listen.

Not My Prayer

by Octavio Solis

Not my prayer but
the daffodils' for sun and bees intoning
in such numbers their fevered mantra
of the morning

not mine but the thousand
prayers of tuna sleek
and silver bursting through the ocean
breach in fear of no net

nor mine the prayers
of dozing lions on the safe road
warming their heaving bodies
sans the unmistakable
scent of hunting humans

all the unkilled bear
deer and song-dog orisons
breathed on roads suddenly still
no speed-of-headlight
death hurtling at them now

all the birdsong more varied
more prayerful than ever
with the chattering of finches common
to our hearing woven
through the calls of species thought
too shy too rare to venture near but here
they are

all the open hemisphere of sky once azure
now azure once again a blue
too blue to fathom except as earth's
petition for just another day
without us

all prayers theirs
for a break from history from this
cult of progress from the unstoppable
momentum of human toil from all this doing and making
from the churning madness of us

praying for a world precipitously devoid
of us long enough for us to grasp
how to their uncomprehending senses
we are the virus itself.

prayers for Big Pookie

by Maya Stein

and the nursing home in Walnut Creek, California where she waits, exiled, behind a numbered door as the casualties mount on the other side. Prayers for her daughter, watching the camera crews prowl the perimeter of the grounds, a sticky palm curled around the phone in her pocket. Prayers for a city seven hundred miles north, finding itself suddenly under siege, and prayers for the yellow-shirted women returning night after night, their arms linked in unshakeable resolve. Prayers for Chicago. Prayers for Minneapolis. Prayers for Nueces, Texas and Calcasieu, Louisiana and Davidson, Tennessee and the bar graphs glowing red and rising. Prayers for what it will take and what will be taken. Prayers for Big Pookie, who could be my grandmother, or yours, whose eyes turn to the window, as all eyes do, searching the clouds for signs.

little prayer

by Danez Smith

let ruin end here

let him find honey
where there was once a slaughter

let him enter the lion's cage
& find a field of lilacs

let this be the healing
& if not   let it be

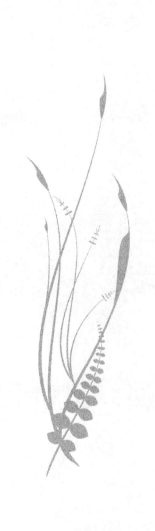

Afterword: Let's Go Forward

by Deborah Jacobs

I find myself obligated to fill this space, to write some closing words when none are necessary, when none are desired, when no words would be a better choice.

I selected Danez Smith's "little prayer" as the closing piece for this issue because I wanted the words, "let ruin end here," to stay with you, to find your heart, to trouble or calm your mind, to hang on the tip of your tongue.

"let ruin end here"
May it be so.

And let's go forward, now, without Afterwords. Let's free up these two pages and commit this space to more words by writers whose voices we absolutely need to hear.

Permissions

Contributors

Elizabeth Alexander is a chancellor of the Academy of American Poets and president of The Andrew W. Mellon Foundation. Her books include *Crave Radiance* and her memoir, *The Light of the World*. In 2009 her poem, "Praise Song for the Day," was commissioned for the inauguration of President Barack Obama.

Rebecca Baggett's poetry appears in journals such as *Miramar*, *New England Review*, *Southern Review*, and *Tar River Poetry*. She is the author of four chapbooks and a full-length collection, *The Woman Who Lives Without Money*, forthcoming from Regal House Publications. She lives in Athens, GA.

Amy Baskin's work is currently featured in *Bear Review*, *River Heron Review*, and is forthcoming in *Pirene's Fountain*. She is a 2019 Pushcart Prize and Best of the Net nominee, a 2019 Oregon Literary Arts Fellow, and a 2019 Oregon Poetry Association prize winner. When she's not writing, she matches international students at Lewis & Clark College with local residents to help them feel welcome and at home during their time in Oregon.

Marvin Bell's most recent book is *Incarnate: The Collected Dead Man Poems*, written over three decades, containing an introductory essay by David St. John. He has published collaborative books with poets William Stafford and Christopher Merrill, photographer

Nathan Lyons, and seven poets from five countries in the single volume *7 Poets, 4 Days, 1 Book*.

Nicole Borg is an English teacher, editor, poet, and poetry cheerleader, who is enamored with place. Her first collection of poetry *All Roads Lead Home* (Shipwreckt Books, 2018) is like a poetry road trip. Nicole lives along the lovely Mississippi River in Minnesota with her husband and two sons.

Jericho Brown won the Pulitzer Prize for his book *The Tradition*.

Lucille Clifton (1936-2010) was a distinguished and decorated American poet. She won the National Book Award for Poetry and was the first Black recipient of the Ruth Lilly Poetry Prize for lifetime achievement. She was named a Literary Lion of New York Public Library in 1996, served as chancellor of the Academy of American Poetry, and was elected a fellow in Literature of the American Academy of Arts and Sciences.

Christopher DeWan is author of *HOOPTY TIME MACHINES: fairy tales for grown ups*, a collection of domestic fabulism from Atticus Books. He lives in Los Angeles and works as a screenwriter, a teacher, and a political activist. Learn more at http://christopherdewan.com.

Brian Doyle (1956-2017) was the author of more than two dozen books—novels, works of nonfiction, and collections of essays, poems, and short stories. His honors include the American Academy of Arts and Letters Award in Literature, the John Burroughs Medal for Distinguished Nature Writing, the Oregon Book Award, and three Pushcart Prizes. A collection of his best spiritual essays, *One Long River of Song*, was published in late 2019.

Ross Gay is the author, most recently, of *Catalog of Unabashed Gratitude* and *The Book of Delights*. His new book, a long poem called *Be Holding*, will be published in September 2020. He works on *The Tenderness Project* with Shayla Lawson and Essence London (tendernesses.com) and teaches at Indiana University.

Joseph Gross writes poems, essays, and stories, some of which have appeared in *Alaska Quarterly Review*, *Fourth Genre*, *Mid-American Review*, *Ninth Letter*, *Redivider*, *Salamander*, *SmokeLong Quarterly*, and others. He is the former Editor-in-Chief of *Atticus Review*, and currently directs a public library in southwestern Michigan, where he lives with his family.

Debra Gwartney is the author of two book-length memoirs, *Live Through This*, a finalist for the National Book Critics Circle Award, and *I Am a Stranger Here Myself*, winner of the River Teeth Nonfiction Prize. She has published in such journals as *Granta*, *American Scholar*, *Tin House*, *The Virginia Quarterly Review*, and in the NYT column, "Modern Love." She teaches in the MFA program at Pacific University and lives in Western Oregon.

Amy Wray Irish grew up in the Chicago area, then relocated to Colorado for the sunshine. Irish received an MFA in Creative Writing from Notre Dame University and has since published two chapbooks: *Creation Stories* (2016) and *The Nature of the Mother* (2019). To read more of her work, check out amywrayirish.com

Michael Kleber-Diggs' writing has appeared in *McSweeney's*, *Pollen Midwest*, *Paper Darts*, *Water~Stone Review* and a few anthologies. Michael is a past Fellow with the Givens Foundation for African-American Literature, a past winner of the Loft Mentor Series in Poetry, and inaugural Poet Laureate of Anoka County Libraries. His work has been supported by the Minnesota State Arts Board, the Jerome Foundation, and the National Endowment for the Arts.

Danusha Laméris' first book, *The Moons of August* (2014) was chosen by Naomi Shihab Nye as the winner of the Autumn House Press poetry prize. Her poems have been published in *The Best American Poetry 2017*, *The New York Times*, *The American Poetry Review*, and elsewhere. Her second book is *Bonfire Opera* (University of Pittsburgh Press, 2020). She teaches poetry independently.

Anna George Meek has published in national journals such as *Poetry*, *The Kenyon Review*, and *The Yale Review*. She is the recipient of an NEA Fellowship, and two Minnesota State Arts

Board grants, and is the author of three prizewinning collections. Meek lives with her husband and daughter in the Twin Cities, where she sings professionally and is a professor of English.

Siri Liv Myhrom is a freelance writer and editor living in Minneapolis, MN. When not writing, she likes to explore her state's remaining wild spaces, in all seasons, with her husband and two young daughters. She has just completed a full-length collection of essays and prose poems on grief called *Even If They Are A Crowd of Sorrows*.

January Gill O'Neil is the author of *Rewilding* (2018), *Misery Islands* (2014), and *Underlife* (2009), published by CavanKerry Press. A Cave Canem fellow, January is an associate professor of English at Salem State University. She lives with her two children in Beverly, Massachusetts.

Danez Smith is the author of *Homie*, (Graywolf Press, 2020), *Don't Call Us Dead* (Graywolf Press, 2017), short-listed for the National Book Award, and *[insert] boy* (YesYes Books, 2014), winner of the Kate Tufts Discovery Award and the Lambda Literary Award for Gay Poetry. The recipient of fellowships from the National Endowment for the Arts and the Poetry Foundation, they are also the winner of a Pushcart Prize and co-host the podcast VS alongside Franny Choi. Smith lives in Minneapolis, Minnesota.

Octavio Solis' newest plays, *Mother Road* and *Quixote Nuevo*, are currently playing in theatres across the country. *Retablos* is his first book.

Maya Stein is a Ninja poet, writing guide, and creative adventuress. Her escapades include a 1,200-mile bicycle journey with a typewriter, a collaboration ("The Creativity Caravan") with her partner, turning a vintage trailer into a mobile workshop and, recently, marriage and step-motherhood. Maya can be found bicycling the backroads and is now, following a stint in suburban New Jersey, happily ensconced in the wilds of mid-coast Maine, in a house named Toad Hall. www.mayastein.com

Rosemerry Wahtola Trommer served as Colorado Western Slope Poet Laureate (2015-2017), co-hosts Emerging Form (a podcast on creative process) and co-directs Telluride's Talking Gourds Poetry Club. Her poetry has appeared in *O Magazine*, on *A Prairie Home Companion* and on river rocks. Her most recent collection, *Hush,* won the Halcyon Prize.
www.wordwoman.com

About the Editor

Deborah Jacobs has been a literature professor, a restaurateur, an arts administrator, and a professional singer; she is also a lifelong road tripper, organic gardener, baseball fan, and indie bookstore loyalist. In October 2018, she founded Danielle Dufy Literary and its imprint, French Press Editions. The mission? To get more short literature that matters into the hands of as many people as possible. To that end, she publishes *Stone Gathering: A Reader* five times a year. Deborah lives in Nisswa, Minnesota with her husband, Bill Ribbel.

Acknowledgements

First thanks, always, to my editorial assistant (and my sister) Michele Jacobs, for her good work and good ideas, her steadfast friendship, and her strong support. To Judith Kissner at Scout & Morgan Books in Cambridge, Minnesota for championing *Stone Gathering* from the beginning, unceasingly and without fail. To Chip and Jean at River Place Press for their generous professionalism, their gorgeous, impeccable layout and design, their kind mentorship, and for the confidence they inspire, issue after issue. To Joey Halvorson for yet another exquisite cover photo. And to Kay at Bang Printing for shepherding these little books home with such care and grace. Finally, thanks to my husband, Bill, for his unwavering belief in me and for the many small and large kindnesses extended as I make my way on this new path.

About French Press Editions

French Press Editions is the publishing imprint of Danielle Dufy Literary, an umbrella company dedicated to celebrating short literature, widening its readership, and supporting independent booksellers.

French Press Editions are small-format (5 x 7), 72-page, perfect-bound paperback books priced at $10.95. They are marketed as *portable, affordable, collectible literature* and are available by subscription and through an increasing number of independent booksellers and other book-friendly establishments.

Stone Gathering: A Reader is a quarterly anthology of previously published short literature intended for a wide audience. Visit our website, www.danielledufy.com, for subscription information and for a list of independent sellers who carry single issues.

Stone Gathering is published 5 times annually. A subscription includes four quarterly issues and a fifth, theme-based special issue. Look for the special issue every year in mid-April.